TAFT
MUSEUM
of ART

An Illustrated Guide

Cincinnati, Ohio

*This publication is made possible
through the generosity of
a friend of the Taft Museum of Art*

All distribution rights belong to: Taft Museum of Art

All Rights Reserved

Text by: Lynne Ambrosini, David T. Johnson, Cate O'Hara, and Abby
Schwartz
All photography by Tony Walsh except p. 44 by Denny Landwehr
Designed by: Don A. Armbruster
Copyright © 2005 The Creative Company
Published by: R. L. Ruehrwein, The Creative Company,
Lawrenceburg, IN 47025
Printed in the U.S.A. on recycled paper with vegetable inks

Cover: Long hall of the Taft Museum of Art
Back cover and page 1: Façade of the Taft Museum of Art
Page 3: Garden and rear elevation of the Taft Museum of Art

Preface

The Taft Museum of Art has seen many changes and alterations since Martin Baum erected this home on what was the edge of town in 1820. Each subsequent owner made additions according to the needs and fashions of the time—updating, expanding, and redecorating. The conversion from a residence to a museum in 1932 introduced more changes and challenges. The most recent expansion and renovation of the museum in 2004 added yet another chapter to that rich and storied history. What remains unchanged, however, is the Taft Museum of Art's place in Cincinnati history as a center for culture, art, and society.

We would like to extend our special thanks to the staff, volunteers, and contractors whose hard work and unstinting attention to detail have created the beautiful interiors, gardens, and installations that visitors enjoy today. From such mundane details as electrical outlets to the stunning new draperies and carpets, each detail contributes to the visitor's experience and serves to highlight the extraordinary masterpieces of fine and decorative art that grace each gallery.

Once the private home of some of Cincinnati's leading citizens, the Taft Museum of Art now welcomes everyone to enjoy and appreciate the works of art on display in its elegantly appointed galleries.

Phillip C. Long
Director, Taft Museum of Art

From House to Museum

From House to Museum

Fig. 1. Nathan Wheeler (American, active about 1815–44), *Martin Baum,* about 1820, oil on canvas. Cincinnati Museum Center, Cincinnati Historical Society Library

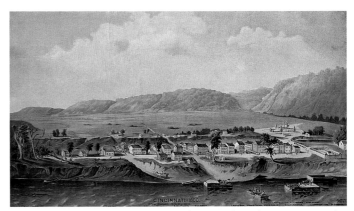

Fig. 2. *Cincinnati—1800,* 1880, color print based on a painting by A. J. Swing. Courtesy of the Merten Company

Contemporaries described it as "the most elegant [house] in town" and "open to all intellectually great men who visited Cincinnati." Unfortunately, Baum, his wife, and their six children lived in it fewer than five years before a national economic crisis forced them to sell it in 1825. Ownership passed to a bank, and a private girls' school rented the space.

Nicholas Longworth (1782–1863) purchased the house in 1829 (fig. 3). In his own words, "I have bought Belmont which is large enough to contain all the Longworths in the

At the eastern edge of downtown Cincinnati, an elegant yet modest white mansion on Pike Street faces the green space of Lytle Park. Around it, a small neighborhood—a sort of time capsule—preserves a number of stately buildings from around 1900. The white house, however, preceded most of them by many decades, having been built in about 1820. A National Historic Landmark, it is listed on the National Register of Historic Places and is signaled in all Cincinnati guidebooks as one of the oldest surviving wooden structures in the city. Although we know it today as the Taft Museum of Art, its full moniker is the Baum-Longworth-Sinton-Taft House, referring to its distinguished roster of former owners.

Martin Baum (1765–1831) had it built but enjoyed it only briefly (fig. 1). Having settled in the "western" frontier town of Cincinnati in the 1790s (fig. 2), Baum prospered initially as a merchant. He eventually owned a sugar refinery, iron foundry, steam mill, and woolen factory and established the first bank in Ohio. He even headed the city's select council as an early, de facto mayor. When he planned the house, he probably hired a local builder who adapted up-to-date neoclassical designs available through architectural handbooks published in the East. The house stood regally on a nine-acre lot and featured a portico (porch framed by columns) that recalled antique Greco-Roman architecture.

Fig. 3. *Nicholas Longworth,* undated, photograph. Cincinnati Museum Center, Cincinnati Historical Society Library

nation." Born in Newark, New Jersey, Longworth had reached Cincinnati as nearly everyone did then, by flatboat down the Ohio River. An enterprising young man, he studied law and accepted land as payment for his legal services, rapidly acquiring substantial property and wealth. In addition to the house on Pike Street, he owned the entirety of Mount Adams and part of Mount Lookout, now separate neighborhoods east of downtown. Eccentric and creative, Longworth terraced the steep hillsides of Mount Adams in order to grow grapes and made one of the first commercial wines in America.

Longworth's other hobby was art. As Cincinnati's first millionaire, he could have simply bought paintings and sculpture: however, this generous patron also supported several talented young artists through their difficult early careers. Among them was the African American landscapist Robert S. Duncanson (1821–1872), from whom Longworth commissioned a suite of eight grand-scale mural paintings to ornament the foyer of the house in about 1850 (see pp. 26–27). Longworth's remarkable support of this young artist sprang in part from his convictions about racial equality: he was an early and ardent abolitionist. Tastes in interior design change, however, and only two decades later the Duncanson murals were covered with wallpaper (fig. 4).

Longworth and his wife were probably responsible for enlarging the house, too, adding side wings to what had

Fig. 4. *Entrance Hall, Taft Residence,* about 1925, photograph. Taft Museum of Art archives

originally been a four-square plan. The earliest known image of the house, an 1857 lithograph commemorating their golden anniversary, shows this wider façade (fig. 5). Soon afterward they added a fanlight and sidelights (overdoor window and side panel windows) to the front door. Luckier than the Baums, Nicholas and Susan Longworth lived in the house for more than thirty years. Indeed, at one point they shared it with six grown offspring and their spouses, fourteen grandchildren, and the family's live-in servants.

Fig. 5. Hunckel & Son, Baltimore, *Belmont* from *Memorial of the Golden Wedding of Nicholas and Susan Longworth Celebrated at Cincinnati on Christmas Eve, 1857,* color lithograph. Taft Museum of Art archives

In 1863, when Longworth died, the house again served briefly as a rental property. The industrialist David Sinton (1808–1900) acquired it in 1871 (fig. 6). He was the third owner of the house to personify the great American rags-to-riches story. Born in Ireland, this thrifty, self-made man began his career in the iron ore industry, then invested in utilities and real estate to amass millions. Sinton's wife died relatively young, leaving him with one surviving child, Anna Sinton (1852?–1931), known as Annie (fig. 7). As a young woman, Annie traveled in Europe with her father. After her marriage in 1873 to Charles Phelps Taft (1843–1929), in an elegant ceremony held in the Music Room—"the great social event of the year in Cincinnati," according to a newspaper account—the young couple settled into the house with Sinton.

Her new husband (fig. 8) came from a prominent family active in law and politics: his father, Alphonso Taft, a lawyer, served as secretary of war in the early 1880s and later undertook diplomatic missions to Vienna and St. Petersburg. Before his marriage Charles earned a law degree from Columbia University and spent two or three years in Europe, completing a doctorate in Germany and then touring the Continent. Back in Cincinnati, a married man, he practiced law. Some years later, he and David Sinton purchased two newspapers that merged to form the Cincinnati *Times-Star*. From this editorial pulpit, Charles Taft supported various cultural, political, and philanthropic causes.

Fig. 8. Raimundo de Madrazo Garreta (Spanish, 1841–1920), *Charles Phelps Taft*, 1902, oil on canvas. Taft Museum of Art

Fig. 7. Raimundo de Madrazo Garreta (Spanish, 1841–1920), *Anna Sinton Taft*, 1902, oil on canvas. Taft Museum of Art

Fig. 9. Joaquín Sorolla y Bastida (Spanish, 1863–1923), *William Howard Taft,* 1909, oil on canvas. Taft Museum of Art

Fig. 10. *Music Room, Taft Residence,* about 1925, photograph. Taft Museum of Art archives

He was active in Republican politics in Ohio, took a seat in the state legislature, served a term in Congress beginning in 1896, and supported his half-brother William Howard Taft in his successful election to the presidency in 1908 (fig. 9). The president-to-be accepted his nomination from the steps of the Pike Street house; the newspaper reported, "The historic porch was decorated with garlands, banners, flags. The thunder of guns and bursting of bombs ushered in the day and the flag was run up in the old Taft garden." For her part, Annie Taft bore and cared for four children; undertook initiatives to improve the quality of education and the arts in Cincinnati, and hosted many glittering parties. The Tafts welcomed many people—artists and politicians, intellectuals

and philanthropists, musicians and visiting literati—to various kinds of social gatherings. They used their main drawing room, the Music Room (fig. 10), and the two side parlors off the foyer to host these events.

The house remained relatively untouched through all this time, although Anna's father, David Sinton, had added a new bedroom wing along the north side. While the Tafts lived in the house, its interiors were papered with patterned wallpapers, its windows and some walls partially masked by heavy velvet draperies, and its rooms filled with an eclectic Victorian mix of French rococo, American federal, and European Renaissance-revival furniture, but the basic bones of the house were preserved (figs. 11, 12).

Fig. 11. *Flemish Library, Taft Residence* (now 19th-Century Figural Painting Gallery), about 1925, photograph. Taft Museum of Art archives

Fig. 12. *Green Room, Taft Residence* (now 19th-Century Landscape and Genre Painting Gallery), about 1925, photograph. Taft Museum of Art archives

In 1900, when David Sinton died, he left his entire fortune—some $15 million—to his daughter, who became the richest woman in Ohio. Together, the Tafts made plans for the enlightened use of their money to support culture and education in the Cincinnati region. In the preceding two decades, they had thrown their already considerable resources behind the creation of the Cincinnati Art Museum. Now they began to travel widely, immerse themselves in the study of art, and collect it magnificently. Admiring the South Kensington Museum and Art School in London, with its emphasis on training in the industrial arts, they determined to purchase art that could elevate the standards of artistic and artisanal production in Cincinnati. Their mission was therefore as much philanthropic as it was aesthetic. They would beautify their home and at the same time share their collection with the public, securing masterpieces to set as educational models before the artists, designers, and leaders of industry in southwestern Ohio. By improving design in manufacturing, they would raise American craftsmanship to the level of European artisanry and thereby enhance their region's economy.

Beginning in 1902 and continuing for almost two decades, the Tafts purchased art from dealers in New York, London, and Paris. Their travels helped to refine their taste for European old master paintings, Chinese porcelains, and European decorative arts. Among paintings, they preferred landscapes and portraits, the genres most popular in America and therefore those that young American artists had to master. By 1928 they had acquired some 700 art objects, consisting primarily of European and American paintings (about 150); antique Chinese ceramics of the Ming and Qing dynasties (about 225); and European decorative arts (about 300), including Limoges enamels, Italian maiolica, and antique watches. Like their fellow Gilded Age collectors, Isabella Stewart Gardner in Boston and Henry Clay Frick in Pittsburgh and New York City, the Tafts set themselves the goal of selecting only works manifesting a supreme level of quality. Notably and distinctively, they also began at the outset to open their house regularly to visitors to share their treasures.

As owners, the only significant change they made to the architecture of the house was to renovate and enlarge the dining room. For this they hired the Cincinnati architects Elzner and Anderson, who in 1910 created a federal-revival breakfast nook separated from the dining room by classical columns. In the main dining room, they installed an ornamental plasterwork ceiling that recalls the work of the British eighteenth-century neoclassical designer Robert Adam (fig.

Fig. 13. *Dining Room, Taft Residence,* about 1925, photograph. Taft Museum of Art archives

13). In 1917 the Tafts had the same firm draw up plans for a two-story picture gallery to be attached to the north bedroom wing, but it was never constructed. During this period, the Tafts also quietly undertook steps to preserve the character of the eastern part of downtown and benefit its working-class residents. They bought some of the older neighboring buildings, founded the Anna Louise Inn for young working women, commissioned the statue of Abraham Lincoln in Lytle Park, and established in it a public playground for poor children.

In 1927 the Tafts turned their attention to the problem of what would become of their collection after their deaths. They decided to bequeath their house, which would serve as a museum, and all their collections to the people of Cincinnati. As they wrote in their 1927 "Deed of Gift," "We desire to devote our collection of pictures, porcelain, and other works of art to the people of Cincinnati in such a manner that they may be readily available to all. We feel that they will be of more value in their present surroundings located in a residence readily accessible to the center of the city and having itself a historical significance in the history of Cincinnati."

Moreover, acting out of their commitment to artistic culture in general, the Tafts leveraged their gift of $1 million to mobilize local support for the arts. They created a foundation called the Cincinnati Institute of Fine Arts, which would endow not only the future museum, but also the Cincinnati Symphony Orchestra and the Cincinnati Opera (both of which Anna Taft had helped to found and fund), the Conservatory of Music, and the Cincinnati Art Museum, if the citizens would raise $2.5 million to contribute, too. They did, and the institute, now called the Fine Arts Fund, continues to set a national model for civic arts fundraising to this day. Annie also established the Charles Taft Memorial Fund for the study of classics and the humanities at the University of Cincinnati with a $2 million endowment. Currently there are over $140 million in endowments for Cincinnati institutions because of the Tafts' largesse.

Charles Taft died in 1929. According to a contemporary, "He was recognized as an internationally known publisher and philanthropist, a quiet man who had helped to spread the fame of Cincinnati. For half a century, artists, writers, musicians, world statesmen, jurists and diplomats, royalty and struggling poets had dined at his board." Anna Taft must have met with Walter P. Siple, the new director of the Cincinnati Art Museum, soon afterward and asked him to oversee the conversion of the house into a museum after her own death. She also told him that there were splendid old murals in the foyer, covered by layers of wallpaper.

When Anna Taft died in 1931, the Cincinnati Art Museum and Eden Park closed to honor her. The newspaper praised "the high plane on which she strove to place our community in music, education, and the fine arts." With her passing, the house on Pike Street ceased to be a home. The Tafts did not wish it to be preserved as a mausoleum, complete with bedside house slippers and reading glasses, but to be entirely renovated in a style appropriate to its federal-period architecture. Most of their belongings went to their children, leaving only the art treasures behind in the new museum.

Walter Siple spent a year renovating and redecorating the house in a federal-revival style resembling that of the early nineteenth century, the period of its creation. The local architectural firm of Garber and Woodward undertook the necessary changes, stripping the house of various anachronistic Victorian features and designing display cases for the ceramics and other small objects (fig. 14). Siple purchased some pieces of fine American neoclassical furniture—sofas, tables, and chairs—to preserve the homey feeling of the future museum. He also hired restorers to strip the wallpaper from the Duncanson murals. Ironically, the layers of paper and glue that had covered them for some sixty years actually helped protect them: they are arguably the most important and well-preserved American pre–Civil War domestic mural suite still in existence. The new Taft Museum opened to the public in November 1932. The community has appreciated it ever since as a special architectural monument on a site full of history and as a repository of superlative art objects to be enjoyed in an intimate, domestically scaled setting.

After operating as a museum for some seventy years without major structural maintenance or updating of its ventilation, plumbing, electricity, or roofing systems, the Taft Museum of Art closed in November 2001 to undergo renovation. This was necessary to protect the building, its collections, and its educational mission—in short, to realize more fully the Tafts' farsighted and beneficent goals.

Fig. 14. *President's Room* (now Barbizon Gallery), 1932, photograph. Taft Museum of Art archives (compare p. 32)

Inside the Taft Museum of Art

Inside the Taft Museum

Each owner of the Baum-Longworth-Sinton-Taft House added to the historic structure and altered its interior decorations. In 1931 founding museum director Walter P. Siple restored the interiors "to provide a dignified backdrop for the Taft collections." He replaced the Tafts' Victorian-era furniture, curtains, wallpapers, moldings, and fireplaces with restrained reproductions and authentic examples from other federal-period houses in the region. Since that systematic restoration, much has changed in the philosophy of architectural restoration and knowledge of nineteenth-century American interiors. Conservators of historic architecture have uncovered earlier layers of paint, wood, and plaster to document more accurately the tastes of the past occupants.

Original texts, designs, and fabrics held in the archives of the Taft Museum of Art attest to the Tafts' aspiration to transform their historic home into a showcase for their art. The museum's 2004 renovation drew upon those resources and current scholarship on American interiors of the nineteenth century. The renovated galleries illustrate the evolution of American interior design during the hundred-year period when the building was a private home. Because few of the original interior design elements survive, federal, Gothic-revival, Renaissance-revival, rococo-revival, Empire-revival, and colonial-revival interiors have been created with reproductions of historically accurate carpeting, window treatments, wallpaper borders, faux graining, and wall colors. The period plasterwork ceilings were conserved and repainted in historic colors.

The décor of each gallery also provides context for the art that it houses. For example, the nineteenth-century Renaissance-revival style has been applied to the gallery that displays works of art from the Renaissance. Throughout, the Tafts' collections have been installed to show the chronological evolution and cross-cultural influences of Chinese, European, and American art from about 750 to 1900 C.E.

Short Hall

Short Hall

This small entrance hall greets visitors to the Taft Museum of Art with a quotation from the deed of gift executed by museum founders Charles and Anna Taft: "We desire to devote our collection of pictures, porcelains, and other works of art to the people of Cincinnati in such a manner that they may be readily available to all."

The few works of art here represent the breadth of their tastes, from the earliest works in the collection, the Chinese Tang dynasty tomb figures dating from about 675–750 C.E. (right), to the then-contemporary sculpture of 1906 by George Gray Barnard (left). This latter work also illustrates the Tafts' desire to support and provide inspiration to living artists.

The early 19th-century design scheme is carried throughout the museum by means of window treatments, wall colors, and carpeting. Appropriate period furnishings, such as this looking glass made in New York in about 1800–1810, were purchased in 1932 to enhance the historic room settings.

This small gallery houses changing exhibitions as well as a sparkling display of forty-nine watches dating from the seventeenth through the nineteenth centuries that once served as visual evidence of the wealth and sophistication of their owners. These mechanical jewels are flanked by a selection of other precious objects, including examples of enameling, goldsmiths' work, and rock crystal carving.

This finely enameled gold watch from France dates from the mid-1600s and illustrates the biblical story from Genesis of Eliezer and Rebecca at the well.

Set with enameled floral still lifes by Hamelin, this diamond-set gold snuffbox was made by goldsmith Jean Ducrollay in Paris in about 1758. The elaboration of the container attests to both the status of its owner and the expense of snuff itself.

This gilded holdback for the sheer cotton curtain was reused from the original 1931 installation of the Taft Museum of Art.

Orientation Gallery

Orientation Gallery

Here visitors are introduced to the former residents of the house: Martin Baum, Nicholas Longworth, David Sinton, and particularly Anna Sinton and Charles Phelps Taft, whose vision and collection shaped the Taft Museum of Art. Family busts of David Sinton (below), Anna's father, and Alphonso Taft (opposite), Charles's father, attest to their pride in their lineage. This gallery is decorated in the classical federal-period (1790–1840) style with an 1840s trellis-patterned Brussels carpet and piped silk valances based on an 1833 design.

The Tafts may have purchased Henry Farny's "Song of the Talking Wire" of 1904 directly from the artist—a testament to their support of local artists. This iconic image of an Indian man with his ear pressed to a telegraph pole expresses the passing of a way of life through the symbolism of the setting sun, snow-covered landscape, and bison skull.

The Tafts' interest in images of the U.S. presidents reflects their commitment to public service. These miniature portraits of George Washington, Thomas Jefferson, Abraham Lincoln, and William Howard Taft (Charles's younger half-brother) are part of a set that includes the first 31 U.S. presidents painted in watercolor on ivory by Arthur J. Rowell and Thomas Lincoln.

Medieval Treasury

During the Middle Ages in Europe, the Catholic Church was the unifying cultural force, influencing the lives of everyone from kings to peasants. The late-medieval and early-Renaissance paintings, tapestry, and decorative arts objects in this gallery are devotional images created for use in churches and, later, private homes or chapels. Intended to evoke a medieval church treasury, the gallery is carpeted with a Gothic-revival design from about 1825 and accented by draperies woven with ornamental, interlaced medieval patterns.

This enameled three-part folding altarpiece was made in France in about 1484–97 by an anonymous master known as Monvaerni. The Crucifixion of Christ is flanked by St. James wearing a traveling cloak to illustrate his role as patron of pilgrims and St. Catherine of Alexandria holding the sword of her martyrdom.

One of the most important surviving medieval ivories, this statue of the Virgin and Child, which dates to about 1260–80, was produced in Paris for the treasury of the Abbey Church of Saint-Denis, the birthplace of Gothic architecture and burial site of French kings.

Renaissance Treasury

Renaissance Treasury

The Renaissance Treasury was inspired by the type of princely Renaissance treasury room known as a *Kunstkammer,* or art chamber. There, nobles displayed small-scale sculpture, coins, medals, and jewelry alongside minerals, zoological specimens, scientific instruments, and medical curiosities. Here, visitors encounter French enamels from Limoges and Italian ceramics together with other rare and precious objects including a Chinese ewer in the shape of a phoenix. This Renaissance-revival interior includes strapwork carpet reproduced from an 1842 design that reflects Limoges enamel patterns. The silk draperies, suspended from crescent moons with star holdbacks, were copied from an early nineteenth-century hand-colored etching in the museum's archives.

This enameled portrait of François de Clèves, duke of Nevers, was made in Limoges, France, in the mid-16th century by Léonard Limosin. The duke commanded the German infantry in the service of King Henry II, rescuing the French army at the battle of Saint-Quentin in 1557.

This "Display Dish with Orpheus Lamenting the Death of Eurydice" was made of maiolica (tin-glazed earthenware) in Faenza, Italy, in about 1520–30 by the eponymous artist called Master of the Taft Orpheus. Costly to produce, maiolica wares were luxury goods in Renaissance Italy.

17th-Century Dutch Gallery

17th-Century Dutch

The rise of a secular merchant class in the Netherlands also gave rise to new forms of art, such as views of everyday middle-class life and landscape views of farms and woodlands. The faux-parquet carpeting in this gallery echoes the inlaid floors found in seventeenth-century Dutch paintings, such as Pieter de Hooch's *A Woman with a Cittern and a Singing Couple at a Table,* visible on the wall to the right. A reproduction of an 1805 French neoclassical textile from the permanent collections has been redesigned as window treatments. Blue-and-white Chinese porcelains are on view here because Dutch trade with China introduced cobalt-decorated ceramics to Europe.

Possibly made as a wedding gift, this charming porcelain box decorated with scrolling flower patterns in underglaze blue enamel is topped with a loop of pine branch and a tiny squirrel. The decorations visually express the wish for a long and happy marriage.

Jan Steen's oil painting "The Doctor's Visit" of about 1663 pokes fun at both the Dutch medical establishment and the swooning woman by means of the booklet on the floor, which reads, "No medicine is of use, for it is lovesickness."

18th-Century British Gallery

During the eighteenth century, the nobility and upper middle class of countries such as England were considerably enriched by a global trading network that included colonies throughout America, Africa, and Asia. British painters such as Thomas Gainsborough and Joshua Reynolds also benefited, receiving numerous commissions for portraits that demonstrated the sitters' social and economic status, as can be seen here. This gallery is decorated in the

federal style influenced by British country houses. The carpet replicating Roman tiles is based on an original design of 1800–1810. The elegant fan-shaped valances of the window treatments are copied from an etching in the museum's archives.

Dating to about 1700, these Chinese porcelain "Buddhistic Lions" bear the Chinese character "wang," an emblem of royal authority, on their foreheads to emphasize the connection of the emperor with Buddhism—marrying politics with religion. Sculptural porcelains of this type were popular with the British upper classes. The Tafts' daughter Louise Taft Semple gave them to the museum in 1948.

In this oil portrait of Mrs. Stephen Payne-Gallwey and her son Charles painted in 1779, Joshua Reynolds demonstrates great tenderness and informality in the maternal relationship. This painting entered the museum in 1962 by bequest from Louise Taft Semple.

19th-Century Landscape and Genre Painting Gallery

The French and English landscapes and genre scenes here illustrate a range of Romantic expressions, including depictions of exotic locales, picturesque views of tourist monuments, imaginary scenes, and mythological subjects, such as J. M. W. Turner's *Europa and the Bull* of about 1840–50 (opposite). The Qing-dynasty porcelains in this gallery include vessels decorated in the famille verte (green family) palette as well as monochromes, or single-color objects,

made for use by China's elite class of scholars. Mirroring the gallery across the Longworth Foyer, this formal parlor is decorated in the late federal/early rococo-revival style. The Greek-revival carpeting with classical medallions is derived from a design dating from about 1827. Silk damask draperies with peplum sides and swag valances are based on a model of 1801 by Thomas Sheraton.

Hanging above a 19th-century American black marble fireplace mantel, Richard Parkes Bonington's oil landscape "View near Mantes" of 1826 displays the artist's characteristic soft brushstrokes, muted color, peaceful riverine subject, low horizon, and small figures that lead the viewer into the pictorial space.

Longworth Foyer

Longworth Foyer

Nicholas Longworth, who owned Belmont, now the Taft Museum of Art, from 1829 to 1863, was a patron of the arts. In about 1850, he commissioned Robert Duncanson, a self-taught African American artist, to decorate his foyer with this suite of eight large landscape paintings and floral overdoor decorations in trompe l'oeil frames. The two busts by Hiram Powers depict museum founder Anna Sinton at age eighteen; on the left is the plaster model that was used to make the final marble bust on the right.

Duncanson's murals are painted in the Hudson River style, which is characterized by Romantic views of virgin landscape. Two idyllic, vaguely European landscapes flank the entryway. The surrounding woodwork, the panels below the chair rail, and the front doors have been faux grained to recreate the domestic setting of the Longworth years.

Duncanson's murals proceeding down the foyer and through the long hall become increasingly picturesque and reminiscent of the Ohio River valley, as in the "Sunset Mural." The eagle vignettes above the arched doorways in the long hall predate Duncanson and were probably painted by an itinerant house painter. The plaster bust of Anna Sinton in the foreground was a gift of Theodore A. Gantz in 1999.

Long Hall

Long Hall

This hallway spans the entire width of the historic house, from north to south. The Duxbury Trellis patterned carpet in gold, white, greens, gray, and raspberry is based on an 1800 design and carries the nineteenth-century federal interior design scheme throughout the house. The two shades of green on the walls are within the family of colors discovered by analysis of early layers of paint.

"Still Life with Tilted Basket of Fruit, Vase of Flowers, and Shells," an oil painting on panel of about 1640–45 by the Dutch master Balthasar van der Ast, is a remarkable composition featuring eight kinds of fruit, 32 species of flowers, 11 seashells, two lizards, three insects, two spiders, and a parrot arranged around a Chinese bowl and a German vase. This painting was a gift of Luther and Josephine Tucker in 2000.

In this small oil panel, "A World of Their Own" of 1905, Lawrence Alma-Tadema positions his young lovers on a flowery plateau above an azure sea. The title, however, may be ironic: while the man has eyes only for the woman, she directs her frank and knowing gaze directly at the viewer.

29

19th-Century Figural Painting Gallery

Charles and Anna Taft acquired their collection of portraits and figural studies both for their own pleasure and to provide models for regional artists. The walls of this formal parlor, which mirrors the décor of the Nineteenth-Century Landscape and Genre Painting Gallery across the Longworth Foyer, are lined with masterpieces by James McNeill Whistler, John Singer Sargent, Jean-Auguste-Dominique Ingres, Frank Duveneck, and others.

An important American realist of the 19th century, Duveneck painted "The Cobbler's Apprentice" in Munich in 1877. His bold, unpretentious style is based on quick brushwork, strong light and dark contrasts, and raw yet picturesque subject matter.

Eighteenth-century peachbloom monochromes (copper-glazed objects for the scholar's table) and famille-rose (opaque enameled ceramics decorated in the pink palette) porcelains from the reigns of the Kangxi, Yongzheng, and Qianlong emperors are also on view in this gallery.

"At the Piano" of 1858–59 is renowned as Whistler's first masterpiece. This picture of the artist's sister and niece is held together visually by a grid of picture frames, moldings, and furniture that unify the composition. It came to the museum as part of the Louise Taft Semple bequest in 1962.

Barbizon School Gallery

Barbizon School Galler

This long gallery houses masterpieces by some of the key artists of the French Barbizon school, so-called for the village in the Forest of Fontainebleau where many of them worked. They rejected the exoticism, exaggerated emotional content, and heroic themes of the Romantic era. Instead, they turned to subjects drawn from the lives of ordinary people and created realistic landscapes, unembellished by mythological or historical themes, often painted outdoors directly from nature. The Chinese porcelains in this gallery are decorated in the famille-noire (black family), famille-jaune (yellow family), and aubergine (dark purple) palettes. The décor of this gallery reconstructs the French Empire taste popular during David Sinton's residency. The Empire block carpeting is based on an 1834 design. The draperies were

inspired by nineteenth-century designs for Rosendal Palace, Sweden.

This marble and gilded bronze mantel clock was made in France in the late 18th century by David-Louis Courvoisier and Jacques-Frédéric Houriet with a movement by L. G. Brocot.

Narcisse Virgile Diaz de la Peña painted "Early Autumn: Forest of Fontainebleau" in 1870. He was a frequent visitor to Barbizon and became an acute observer of the seasonal and meteorological changes that made the region attractive to landscape painters.

Dining Room

Dining Room

In 1910 Anna and Charles Taft commissioned a local architectural firm to enlarge and renovate their dining room in a neoclassical style inspired by the eighteenth-century British architects Robert and James Adam. This style is evident in the plasterwork ceiling that was installed at that time. The serene landscapes are by painters of the French Barbizon school. The invention of the collapsible tin paint tube in the 1840s made it easier for artists to paint out of doors—*en plein air*—where they could observe and capture effects of light and weather.

A pair of columns that once separated this breakfast alcove from the main dining area was removed during the 1931 renovation of the museum from a private home. (Compare fig. 13 on page 9.)

Charles-François Daubigny had a floating studio boat from which to paint his beautiful riverscapes, including "A River Scene: The Ferry at Bonnières" of 1861.

The mahogany sideboard, dining table, and set of side chairs were made in New York in the first quarter of the nineteenth century. Their neoclassical design harmonizes with that of the plasterwork ceiling medallion. The Turkish-style carpet is based on a design of 1913 and is similar to the rug that the Tafts had in this room during their residency.

To make the blue background, powdered cobalt was blown onto this Chinese rouleau vase of about 1700 through a piece of gauze stretched over the end of a bamboo tube. The scenes enameled in famille verte depict episodes from "The Romance of the Western Chamber," a popular 14th-century Chinese novel.

Hague School Gallery

Hague School Gallery

Once a butler's pantry, this tiny gallery houses paintings by late nineteenth-century Dutch artists, known collectively as the Hague school, who specialized in landscapes and scenes of daily life. They also experimented with painting outdoors, like their earlier French counterparts, the Barbizon painters. They executed their paintings using light tones and loose, expressive brushwork, often applying thick layers of pigment to achieve textural effects.

Recognized as one of the great artists of the Hague school, Jan Hendrik Weissenbruch used a direct, spontaneous style to convey the damp northern climate in "A Gray Day in Holland" of 1899.

Music Room

Music Room

The Music Room has been refurbished in a late federal/early rococo-revival style, with reproduction 1830s carpeting as well as draperies recreated from 19th-century designs published in France. This style is characterized by S-shaped curves, bright colors accented with gold, and the harmonious combination of naturalistic motifs, such as the design of peonies in the carpet.

The magnificent Music Room remains the most important room in the historic house. Once the site of glittering receptions and celebrations of all sorts, including the wedding of Charles Taft and Anna Sinton in 1873, it now houses some of the museum's finest European old master paintings, Chinese porcelains, and European decorative arts, highlighting the fields of art that the Tafts collected. Seen (opposite) in his portrait by Raimundo de Madrazo (1902), Charles Phelps Taft gazes from above the fireplace at portraits by Frans Hals (left and right) and Thomas Gainsborough (center).

Among the masterpieces of art in the Music Room are Rembrandt's "Portrait of a Man Rising from His Chair" of 1633 (left), "Portrait of a Man" painted by Frans Hals in about 1632–34, and two mid-18th-century French commodes by Pierre Roussel.

From above the fireplace, Anna Sinton Taft reigns from her 1902 portrait by Madrazo over landscapes by Meyndert Hobbema, Thomas Gainsborough, and J. M. W. Turner (left to right).

These three monumental pictures illustrate the evolution of landscape painting through the seventeenth, eighteenth, and nineteenth centuries.

Among many examples of Chinese porcelain in the Music Room, this blue-and-white baluster vase of about 1700 is decorated with a scene from the Song dynasty novel "The Generals of the Yang Family," in which women train to fight foreign invaders after the men have fallen in battle.

This classical sofa was made in New York in about 1815–25 possibly by Michael Allison. It is upholstered in magenta silk with gold rosettes.

New Wing, 2004

New Wing, 2004

Visitors to the Taft Museum of Art now enter the building through the Dr. Stanley and Mickey Kaplan Lobby. The curved staircase leads invitingly to a light-filled space that looks out onto the garden. The Carl and Edyth Lindner Tea Room offers refreshment and respite with both indoor and outdoor seating on the Harold C. Schott Foundation Terrace. The Museum Shop extends the museum experience with appropriate gifts and books related to the Taft collections, exhibitions, and history.

Luther Hall
Luther Hall

Luther Hall and the adjacent Farmer Family Lobby provide a versatile space for lectures, recitals, performances, receptions, corporate functions, and private parties of all kinds. The Fifth Third Bank Special Exhibitions Gallery is host to a series of changing special exhibitions that relate in diverse ways to the museum's permanent collections.

Fifth Third Gallery

Fifth Third Gallery

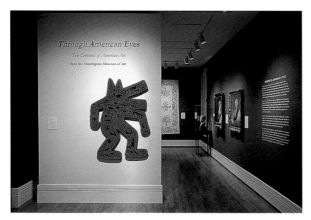

Rowe Family Garden

Rowe Family Garden

The rectilinear plan and green and white color scheme of the Rowe Family Garden complement the clean lines of the American Palladian architecture, illustrated by the rows of columns supporting the rear portico. The garden is divided into four areas: a formal garden with a central panel of grass, walkways, and beds with an overall white planting scheme; a woodland area with dogwood and curving paths; a terrace for outdoor dining under the cherry trees; and a large brick-paved terrace for special events.

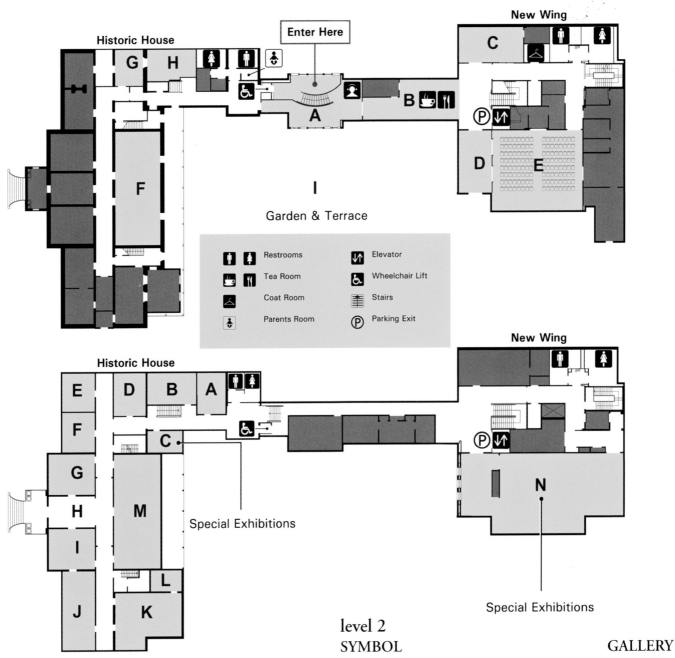

Enter Here

Historic House

New Wing

G H

C

A

B

I

Garden & Terrace

D E

F

Restrooms

Elevator

Tea Room

Wheelchair Lift

Coat Room

Stairs

Parents Room

Parking Exit

Historic House

New Wing

E D B A

F

C

G

M

Special Exhibitions

H

I

L

N

J K

Special Exhibitions

level 1

SYMBOL	SPACE
A	Kaplan Lobby (Admission/Audio Tours)
B	Tea Room
C	Museum Shop
D	Farmer Family Lobby
E	Luther Hall
F	Dater Education Room*
G	Corbett Educator Resource Center*
H	Library*
I	Rowe Family Garden

* Access by appointment only

level 2

SYMBOL	GALLERY
A	Orientation Gallery
B	Medieval Treasury
C	Keystone Gallery
D	Renaissance Treasury
E	17th-Century Dutch
F	18th-Century British
G	19th-Century Landscape & Genre
H	Longworth Foyer
I	19th-Century Figural Painting
J	Barbizon School
K	Dining Room
L	Hague School
M	Music Room
N	Fifth Third Gallery